From T

WELCOME to **100 Ultimate Cocktails** – your comprehensive guide to the world of cocktails. Whether you're a seasoned connoisseur or a curious enthusiast, we hope this curated collection of exquisite drinks will help you find some holiday inspiration, demystify some of the techniques behind the mixing, and lead you on a path to your new favourite cocktail.

From timeless classics to avant-garde creations, this is your passport to the most celebrated and sought-after cocktails in existence.

We'll also cover the barware you need, the world's most expensive cocktails, the humour you can inject into your menu, and cocktail and food pairings that will enhance any dining experience.

It's time now for you to embark on a sensational journey through a comprehensive list of exquisite drinks that span the globe, each with its own unique story and flair. Cheers!

Welcome

SHAKEN, STIRRED AND STORIED
A HISTORY OF COCKTAILS

EARLY BEGINNINGS	16TH-18TH CENTURY	19TH CENTURY	PROHIBITION ERA (1920-1933)	MODERN MIXOLOGY	GLOBAL INFLUENCE
The idea of blending alcohol with various components has roots in ancient civilizations. Egyptians, Greeks, and Romans combined wine with herbs, honey, and spices not only for medicinal reasons but also to enrich the taste. During medieval times in Europe, a blend of alcohol with herbs and spices was utilised to produce medicinal potions. These early mixtures laid the foundation for modern cocktails.	During the 16th and 17th centuries, punch gained popularity among British sailors and settlers. This beverage, usually consisting of a blend of spirits, sugar, lemon, water, and tea or spices, represented an early example of a shared cocktail experience. The term "cocktail" was officially documented in an American publication in 1806, described as "a stimulating drink made with spirits, sugar, water, and bitters".	In the 19th century, the emergence of skilled bartenders elevated cocktails to a refined option. This era saw the birth of iconic cocktails like the Martini, Manhattan, and Old Fashioned. The introduction of bitters and a wider range of ingredients enhanced the intricacy of these beverages, marking a significant evolution in cocktail culture.	During the Prohibition era in the United States, where alcohol sale and consumption were prohibited, numerous American bartenders relocated to Europe, exporting their expertise in crafting cocktails and leaving a lasting impact on drinking traditions overseas. This period gave birth to several legendary cocktails such as the French 75 and the Bee's Knees.	In the late 20th and early 21st centuries, there has been a revival in cocktail culture, focusing on craftsmanship, originality, and inventiveness. Contemporary mixologists venture into the realm of molecular gastronomy, utilise fresh organic ingredients, and incorporate artisanal spirits to craft cutting-edge and imaginative beverages.	The world of cocktails has been shaped by a fusion of international tastes, incorporating elements from diverse culinary traditions like Japanese yuzu, Peruvian pisco, and Indian spices. Current trends highlight a commitment to sustainability, where mixologists prioritise locally sourced ingredients. Additionally, there is a growing demand for low-alcohol and non-alcoholic cocktails.

Contents

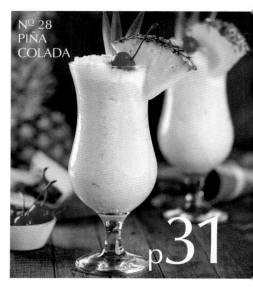

№ 28
PIÑA COLADA

p31

№ 49
SPICY MARGARITA

p54

p47

№ 43
CLOVER CLUB

p79

Nº 72
GRASSHOPPER

Nº 57
GINGERBREAD
MARTINI

p64

Nº 38
AVIATION

p42

Nº 64
MULLED
WINE

p71

US Measurement Conversions

Spoons and cups to ml

1/4 tsp = 1.25ml
1/2 tsp = 2.5ml
1 tsp = 5ml
1 tbsp = 15ml
1/4 cup = 60ml
1/3 cup = 80ml
1/2 cup = 125ml
1 cup = 250ml

Note: These measurements are for guidance only. For precise measurements, we suggest using an online conversion tool.

Gareth Whelan: Editorial Director
Jaclyn Bryson: Head of Design
Peter McDonald: Head of Production

Contact: lifestyleseries@dcthomson.co.uk

Images throughout: Shutterstock unless otherwise stated.

ipso. Regulated

DC THOMSON

Ingredients
60ml vodka
120ml tomato juice
1tbsp lemon juice
2-4 dashes Worcestershire sauce
2-4 dashes hot sauce (eg Tabasco)
Pinch of celery salt
Pinch of black pepper
2.5ml horseradish (optional)
Large handful of ice
Celery stalk and lime wedge (optional)
Ice cubes

Method
● Rim the glass with celery salt by running a lemon wedge around the rim and dipping it in celery salt.
● Fill the glass with ice.
● In a shaker, combine the vodka, tomato juice, lemon juice, Worcestershire sauce, hot sauce, horseradish, celery salt and pepper.
● Shake well and strain into the glass over ice.
● Garnish with a celery stalk, if using, and lime wedge.
● Stir and enjoy!

Bloody Mary

A Bloody Mary is one of the world's most famous cocktails, known for its ability to kick-start even the sleepiest of mornings.

SOMETHING ABOUT MARY

● The vibrant flavours of this fresh drink have been a firm favourite for generations. Whether enjoyed with a lavish brunch or downed as a hangover remedy, this versatile libation has secured its place as a staple in cocktail culture.

● Restaurants and bars have been vying to come up with the most creative twist to the recipe, topping their versions with everything from bacon to lobster tails. But most people love it with no frills – you can't beat a classic!

● The Bloody Mary's staying power and ongoing appeal is easy to see. After all, it's one of the few cocktails that is socially acceptable to drink first thing in the morning. What else needs to be said?

Martini

Ingredients
60ml gin
15ml dry vermouth
1 dash orange bitters
Lemon twist or olive
Ice cubes

Method
● Add the gin, dry vermouth and orange bitters into a mixing glass with ice and stir gently until very cold.
● Strain into a chilled cocktail glass.
● Garnish with a lemon twist or olive.

Don't cut corners on the quality of ingredients and unlike the demands of James Bond, a martini is meant to be stirred, not shaken!

Manhattan

Ingredients

50ml whisky (usually bourbon or rye)
25ml sweet vermouth
2-3 dashes Angostura bitters
Maraschino cherry
Ice cubes

Method

● Fill a mixing glass with ice. Add whisky, sweet vermouth, and Angostura bitters. Stir well to chill the mixture and dilute slightly.
● Strain the cocktail into a chilled Martini glass or over ice in a rocks glass.
● Garnish with a maraschino cherry.
● Serve and savour the classic sophistication of a Manhattan cocktail. Enjoy!

The Manhattan cocktail is believed to have originated at the Manhattan Club in New York City in the 1870s.

Old Fashioned

Dating back to America in the early 19th-century the Old Fashioned is recognised as one of the world's first cocktails.

Ingredients

2tsp sugar syrup or 1tsp granulated sugar
2 dashes Angostura bitters
Ice cubes
60ml whisky or bourbon
Soda water (optional)
Orange slice
Maraschino cherry (optional)

Method

● Put the sugar, bitters and a splash of water in a small mixing glass. Mix until the sugar dissolves if using granulated.
● Fill your glass with ice and stir in the whisky.
● Add a splash of soda water, if you like, and mix. Garnish with the orange and cherry.

The salt on the glass's rim is important as it brings out the sweet and sour flavours of the drink and helps to subdue the bitterness.

Ingredients
50ml tequila reposado
25ml lime juice
20ml triple sec
Salt
Lime wedges
Ice cube

Method
● Sprinkle a salt over the surface of a small plate or saucer. Rub one wedge of lime along the rim of a glass and then dip the glass into the salt so that the entire rim is covered.
● Fill a cocktail shaker with ice, then add the tequila, lime juice and triple sec. Shake until the outside of the shaker feels cold.
● Strain the mix into the prepared glass over fresh ice. Serve with a wedge of lime.

Margarita

Mojito

A Cuban classic, this cocktail now has worldwide appeal and is the most popular on any drinks menu!

Ingredients
50ml white rum
25ml fresh lime juice
12.5ml simple syrup
(or 2tsp granulated sugar)
6-8 fresh mint leaves
Soda water
Sprig of mint
Lime wedge
Ice cubes

Method
● In a glass, muddle the mint leaves with lime juice and simple syrup.
● Fill the glass with ice. Pour in the rum and stir well.
● Top up with soda water. Garnish with a mint sprig and lime wedge.
● Stir gently and enjoy the refreshing taste. Cheers!

Negroni

The Negroni cocktail, created in Florence, Italy, in the early 20th century, is celebrated for its elegant balance of gin, vermouth, and Campari, a timeless Italian classic.

Ingredients
25ml gin
25ml sweet vermouth
25ml Campari
Orange slice
Ice cubes

Method
● Fill a mixing glass with ice.
● Add gin, sweet vermouth and Campari.
● Stir well to combine and chill the mixture.
● Strain the cocktail into a rocks glass filled with ice.
● Garnish with an orange slice, and serve.

Ingredients
50ml white rum
25ml fresh lime juice
12.5ml simple syrup
(or 2tsp sugar)
Lime wedge
Fresh mint
Ice cubes

Method
- Fill a shaker with ice.
- Add white rum, fresh lime juice, and simple syrup (or granulated sugar) and shake well until chilled.
- Strain into a chilled Martini or coupe glass.
- Garnish with a lime wedge and sprig of mint.

Although simple in terms of number of ingredients, it's important to get the balance correct when making to ensure none of the elements overpower the others.

Daiquiri

Whisky Sour

A barspoon of red wine added to your Whisky Sour can give the drink a delicious warmth help to balance out the flavours.

Ingredients
50ml whisky
25ml fresh lemon juice
12.5ml simple syrup
(or 2tsp granulated sugar)
Dried citrus slice
Pomegranate seeds
Ice cubes

Method
● Fill a shaker with ice.
● Add whisky, fresh lemon juice, and simple syrup. Shake well to chill the mixture.
● Strain into a rocks glass filled with ice. Garnish with the dried citrus slice and a scattering of the pomegranate seeds.
● Serve, and enjoy the zesty smoothness.

Tom Collins

Ingredients
50ml gin
25ml fresh lemon juice
12.5ml simple syrup
Soda water
Lemon slice
Cherry
Ice cubes

A Tom Collins is a warm weather treat. Tasting like spiked lemonade, it provides everything you need to cool down on a hot summer afternoon.

Method
● Fill a shaker with gin, fresh lemon juice, and simple syrup.
● Shake well with ice and strain into a tall glass filled with ice.
● Top up with soda water. Stir gently to mix.
● Garnish with a lemon slice and a cherry.

Moscow Mule

Make an autumn-inspired version by adding 30ml of apple and cranberry juice and swapping the lime slices and mint for fresh apple and cranberries.

Ingredients
50ml vodka
120ml ginger beer
15ml fresh lime juice
Lime slices
Mint
Ice cubes

Method
● Pour the vodka, lime juice into a mule mug, highball glass, or rocks glass with ice and stir briefly to combine.
● Top with ginger beer.
● Garnish with lime slice and fresh mint.

Gin Fizz

To add a layer of foam to the top of the glass, this tipple needs both a dry shake (without ice) and a wet shake (with ice) to help merge all the ingredients perfectly.

Ingredients

60ml gin
22ml fresh lemon juice
30ml simple syrup
1 egg white
Club soda
Sprig of thyme
Slice of lemon
Ice cubes

Method

● In a shaker, combine the gin, lemon juice, simple syrup, and egg white.
● Dry shake (without ice) for about 15 seconds.
● Add ice to the shaker and shake again for another 30 seconds.
● Strain the mixture into a glass without ice.
● Top off with club soda.
● Garnish with a sprig of thyme and slice of lemon.

Cosmopolitan

Ingredients
45ml lemon vodka
15ml Cointreau
10ml lime juice
30ml cranberry juice
Ice cubes

Method
● Add the vodka, Cointreau, lime juice and cranberry juice cocktail into a shaker with ice and shake until well chilled.
● Strain into a chilled cocktail glass.
● Garnish with a twist of lime.

The Cosmopolitan, known for its vibrant pink colour, gained popularity in the late '90s thanks to its association with the TV show *Sex And The City*.

Mint Julep

The word julep was used as early as the late 14th century to refer to "a syrupy drink in which medicine was given".

Ingredients
75ml bourbon
15ml simple syrup
Fresh mint leaves
Crushed ice

Method
● In a glass or julep cup, muddle a few mint leaves with the simple syrup.
● Fill the glass with crushed ice.
● Add bourbon and stir well to combine.
● Top with more crushed ice.
● Garnish with a sprig of mint.

Pisco Sour

Victor Vaughen Morris, an American who moved to Peru in 1903 for the mining trade, opened a bar called Morris Bar and it was there he made the first Pisco Sour as an alternative to the Whisky Sour.

Ingredients
50ml Pisco
25ml fresh lime juice
20ml simple syrup
1 egg white
Angostura bitters
Ice Cubes

Method
● Add Pisco, lime juice, simple syrup, and egg white to a shaker.
● Dry shake (without ice) for 15 seconds.
● Add ice to the shaker and shake vigorously for around 30 seconds.
● Strain into a glass. Add a few drops of Angostura bitters on top.

Sidecar

The Sidecar is believed to have originated in Paris during World War I and is indeed named after the motorcycle accessory!

Ingredients
50ml Cognac
25ml triple sec
25ml fresh lemon juice
Sugar to rim the glass
(optional)
Citrus twist
Ice cubes

Method
● Rim a chilled glass with sugar.
● In a shaker, combine the Cognac, triple sec, and lemon juice.
● Fill the shaker with ice and shake well.
● Strain into the prepared glass.
● Garnish with a citrus twist.

French 75

This cocktail is named after the portable and fast firing 75-millimetre field gun that was used by the French during World War I.

Ingredients

25ml gin
15ml fresh lemon juice
10ml simple syrup
Champagne (or sparkling wine)
Lemon twist
Ice cubes

Method

● In a shaker, combine the gin, lemon juice and simple syrup.
● Fill the shaker with ice and shake well until chilled.
● Strain into a Champagne flute. Top up with Champagne.
● Garnish with a lemon twist.

Caipirinha

Originating in Brazil, the Caipirinha is pronounced "kai-pur-reen-yah" which translates as "little countryside drink".

Ingredients
50ml Cachaça
Half a lime, cut into wedges
2tsps white sugar
Crushed ice

Method
● Place lime wedges and sugar in a glass.
● Muddle well to release the lime juice.
● Fill the glass with crushed ice.
● Pour Cachaça over the ice and stir well to combine.

Mai Tai

Lots of crushed ice is key here! Use too little and it melts quicker leaving a weak and watery cocktail.

Ingredients
50ml dark rum
25ml white rum
15ml orange curaçao
15ml orgeat syrup
25ml fresh lime juice
Sprig of mint
Pineapple wedge

Method
● Fill a shaker with ice. Add both rums, orange curaçao, orgeat syrup, and lime juice.
● Shake well and strain into a glass filled with crushed ice.
● Garnish with mint and pineapple wedge.

Bee's Knees

Many believe this cocktail was invented during Prohibition in the United States with the lemon juice and honey syrup used to mask the flavour of cheap bathtub gin!

Ingredients
50ml gin
20ml honey syrup (mix equal parts honey and hot water)
20ml fresh lemon juice
Crystallised ginger

Method
● In a shaker, combine the gin, honey syrup, and lemon juice.
● Fill the shaker with ice and shake well.
● Strain into a glass.
● Garnish with a cube of crystallised ginger.

Aperol Spritz

While the low alcohol Aperol Spritz has been enjoyed in Italy for more than a century, it didn't reach mass appeal in the United States until the 2010s.

Ingredients
60ml Aperol
90ml prosecco
Splash of soda water
Orange slice
Ice cubes

Method
● Fill a wine glass with ice cubes.
● Add the Aperol, followed by prosecco.
● Top off with a splash of soda water.
● Stir gently to combine.
● Garnish with an orange slice.

Espresso Martini

The three coffee beans that should garnish your Espresso Martini represent health, wealth and happiness.

Ingredients
50ml vodka
25ml coffee liqueur
25ml freshly brewed espresso
10ml sugar syrup
Ice cubes

Method
● Fill a shaker with ice.
● Add vodka, coffee liqueur, espresso and sugar syrup.
● Shake vigorously until well-chilled.
● Strain into a Martini glass.
● Garnish with coffee beans.

Mimosa

Mimosas are such a popular cocktail they have their own holiday! May 16 is National Mimosa Day – be sure to celebrate!

Ingredients
75ml chilled Champagne or sparkling wine
75ml fresh orange juice
Orange twist or wedge

Method
● Pour chilled Champagne or sparkling wine into a flute glass.
● Top up with fresh orange juice. Gently stir to combine.
● Garnish with an orange twist or wedge.

Ingredients

60ml tequila
90ml grapefruit soda
15ml fresh lime juice
Salt
Grapefruit slice
Thyme
Ice cubes

Method

- If desired, rim a glass with salt.
- Fill the glass with ice.
- Add tequila and fresh lime juice.
- Top up with grapefruit soda.
- Stir gently to mix.
- Garnish with a grapefruit slice and a thyme sprig.

This delightful and refreshing tequila-based cocktail has become a staple of Mexico's culinary culture, pairing well with Mexican cuisine.

Paloma

Shaken, Stirred And Surprising

Check out these fascinating cocktail facts!

The most ordered cocktail in the world is the Margarita.

■ The Sourtoe Cocktail in Dawson City, Canada, contains a mummified human toe that has been dehydrated, preserved in salt and used to garnish!

■ In the midst of Prohibition in the United States, a clandestine world of hidden bars, known as speakeasies, flourished across the nation. The term speakeasy traces its roots to a clever female bartender who hushed unruly patrons by whispering, "speak easy, boy, speak easy", keeping the secret venues safe from prying eyes and avoiding detection.

■ Never mind using gin in their cocktails, in the early 20th century, Russians instead used the drink as a remedy for arthritis by rubbing it on their joints and then wrapping them in bear skins.

While it's not made our list, there is such a cocktail as the Bubble Bath Martini which is often garnished with a mini rubber duck!

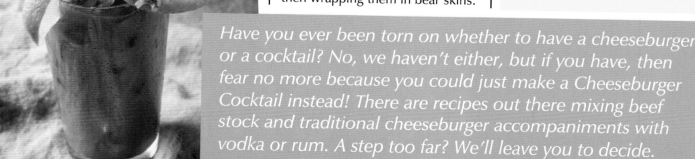

Have you ever been torn on whether to have a cheeseburger or a cocktail? No, we haven't either, but if you have, then fear no more because you could just make a Cheeseburger Cocktail instead! There are recipes out there mixing beef stock and traditional cheeseburger accompaniments with vodka or rum. A step too far? We'll leave you to decide.

World Cocktail Day is a global celebration of cocktails and takes place every year on May 13.

The White Russian cocktail is associated with "The Dude" from the 90s Coen Brothers comedy The Big Lebowski. The character, played by Jeff Bridges, is seen drinking White Russians throughout the film.

■ In July 2012, Nick Nicora from the United States set a Guinness World Record for the largest cocktail ever made with a 10,499 gallon Margarita!

■ In 2014 in celebration of the Commonwealth Games in Glasgow, a Commonwealth Cocktail was created which had a total of 71 ingredients to honour each country competing at the games!

■ The most cocktails made in one hour is 1,905 and was achieved by Sheldon Wiley at the Bounce Sporting Club in New York in 2014. That sure is quick service!

■ The term "happy hour" originated in the United States Navy in the 1920s. It was used to describe a scheduled period of entertainment on board ships during which sailors could enjoy various activities to relieve stress and boost morale. Over time, the term transitioned to refer to a period in bars or restaurants offering discounted drinks to attract customers during off-peak hours.

■ One of the theories behind people clinking their glasses during a toast is that the clinking sound would ward off evil spirits. Others believe it dates back to when people often tried to poison each other. If a host wanted to prove that their drink wasn't poisoned, they would pour part of the guest's drink into their own glass and drink it first. If the guest trusted his host, they would just clink glasses when the host offered his glass for a sample thus becoming a sign of trust, honesty and good health.

A Bloody Mary is a popular choice of cocktail to drink while on an airplane. Participants of a 2016 study had trouble picking out sweet flavours in a noisy airplane environment, but found it easier to taste savoury flavours, just like those present in tomatoes.

27

A Tequila Sunrise appears exotic, but is just a simple three-ingredient recipe and is deliciously refreshing. For smooth sipping, ensure the ingredients are fresh and high quality.

Tequila Sunrise

RISE TO THE OCCASION

● The Tequila Sunrise has its roots in the early 20th century at a hotel resort in Arizona, where tequila's popularity was taking off in the United States after the end of the Mexican Revolution.

● The sweet, refreshing drink gained fame in the '70s, becoming synonymous with laidback vibes and beach days. Its popularity soared, especially among music enthusiasts. The Rolling Stones famously developed a thirst for the cocktail on their 1972 tour which further propelled its allure. The Eagles had a top 40 hit with the song *Tequila Sunrise*.

● Although it's now widely customised, a classic Tequila Sunrise is a delicious taste of nostalgia. Carefully pouring the grenadine down the glass creates the evocative gradient that gives it its name.

Ingredients
50ml tequila
100ml orange juice
15ml grenadine syrup
Ice cubes
Orange or lime slices

Method
● Fill a glass with ice.
● Pour in tequila and orange juice.
● Stir gently to mix.
● Slowly pour grenadine down the side of the glass for the sunrise effect.
● Garnish with a citrus slice.

Zombie

This cocktail was originally invented in the 1930s aiming to cure hangovers. Unfortunately, the high-alcohol blend left the recipient feeling like a "zombie"!

Ingredients

50ml white rum
50ml dark rum
25ml lime juice
25ml pineapple juice
25ml apricot brandy
15ml grenadine
1 dash of bitters
Crushed ice
Lime wedges

Method

● Fill a shaker with crushed ice.
● Add all the rums, lime juice, pineapple juice, apricot brandy, grenadine, and bitters.
● Shake well then strain into a glass filled with crushed ice.
● Garnish with a wedge of lime.

Hurricane

After World War II, spirits like bourbon and whisky were in short supply. Thankfully, rum was plentiful, which forced bartenders to get creative and led to new cocktails such as the Hurricane.

Ingredients

50ml dark rum
50ml white rum
50ml passion fruit juice
25ml orange juice
25ml lime juice
15ml simple syrup
15ml grenadine
Ice cubes
Lime slices

Method

● Fill a shaker with ice.
● Add the dark rum, white rum, passion fruit juice, orange juice, lime juice, simple syrup, and grenadine.
● Shake well. Strain into a glass filled with ice.
● Garnish with a lime slice.

Piña Colada

The name Piña Colada translates directly from Spanish as "strained pineapple". Created in San Juan, it's so popular that it was made Puerto Rico's national drink in 1978.

Ingredients

50ml white rum
100ml pineapple juice
50ml coconut cream
10ml fresh lime juice
Crushed ice
Pineapple wedges and maraschino cherries

Method

● In a blender, combine the white rum, pineapple juice, coconut cream, lime juice, and ice.
● Blend until smooth. Pour into a glass.
● Garnish with a pineapple wedge and cherry.

Bahama Mama

Ingredients
25ml dark rum
25ml coconut rum
25ml pineapple juice
25ml orange juice
10ml grenadine
10ml lemon juice
Ice cubes
Orange slices and cherries

Method
● Fill a shaker with ice.
● Add dark rum, coconut rum, pineapple juice, orange juice, grenadine, and lemon juice.
● Shake well. Strain into a glass filled with ice.
● Garnish with an orange slice and cherry.

The Bahama Mama cocktail does not have a standard recipe, but it has two popular variations. One features the distinctive taste of coffee liqueur, while this recipe features grenadine and has a sweeter flavour and bright colour.

Blue Lagoon

Ingredients
50ml vodka
25ml blue curaçao
150ml lemonade
Ice cubes
Lime slices

Method
● Fill a glass with ice.
● Pour the vodka and blue curaçao over the ice.
● Top up with lemonade.
● Stir gently to combine.
● Garnish with a lime slice.

The vodka base is complemented by blue curaçao, a Caribbean liqueur crafted from the dried peel of the Laraha citrus fruit and tinted blue, offering sweet and zesty flavours.

Singapore Sling

Ingredients
40ml gin
15ml cherry brandy
7.5ml Cointreau
7.5ml D.O.M. Bénédictine
120ml pineapple juice
15ml lime juice
10ml grenadine
A dash of Angostura bitters
Soda water
Ice cubes
Orange slices and maraschino cherries

Method
● Fill a shaker with ice.
● Add the gin, cherry brandy, Cointreau, D.O.M. Bénédictine, pineapple juice, lime juice, grenadine, and bitters.
● Shake well and strain into a glass with ice.
● Top with soda water.
● Garnish with a pineapple slice and cherry.

You can still order a Singapore Sling at its birthplace in the lap of luxury at Raffles Hotel in Singapore. If that's out of budget, homemade can be just as good!

Planter's Punch

While this classic Planter's Punch is a delight, it's worth experimenting with different types of rum, like white or spiced, to find your preferred taste.

Ingredients

50ml dark rum
25ml fresh lime juice
15ml grenadine
10ml sugar syrup
Dash of Angostura bitters
Soda water
Ice cubes
Lime slices and strawberries

Method

● Fill a glass with ice.
● Add the dark rum, lime juice, grenadine, sugar syrup, and bitters.
● Stir well and then top up with soda water.
● Garnish with a lime slice and strawberry.

Painkiller

Ingredients
50ml dark rum
25ml coconut cream
75ml pineapple juice
25ml orange juice
Ice cubes
Grated nutmeg
Pineapple wedges

Method
- Fill a shaker with ice.
- Add the dark rum, coconut cream, pineapple juice, and orange juice.
- Shake well and then strain into a glass filled with ice.
- Garnish with grated nutmeg and pineapple wedge.

Just like its namesake, this cocktail is the perfect cure for what ails you! The coconut cream adds a smooth sweetness, making this perfect for Piña Colada fans.

Sex On The Beach

Believed to have been first created in Florida during the 1980s, this cocktail's attention grabbing name has made it a go-to beachside beverage.

Ingredients
50ml vodka
25ml peach schnapps
50ml cranberry juice
50ml orange juice
Ice cubes
Lime or orange slices

Method
● Fill a glass with ice.
● Add vodka and peach schnapps.
● Pour in cranberry juice and orange juice.
● Stir gently to mix.
● Garnish with a citrus slice.

While this recipe is served on the rocks, the ingredients can also be blended with ice for a creamy, smooth texture. Perfect for hot summer days by the pool.

Ingredients
50ml white rum
25ml blue curaçao
50ml pineapple juice
25ml coconut cream
10ml fresh lime juice
Ice cubes
Mint leaves, lemon slices and blueberries

Method
● Fill a shaker with ice.
● Add the white rum, blue curaçao, pineapple juice, coconut cream, and lime juice.
● Shake well and strain into a glass filled with ice.
● Garnish with a pineapple slice and cherry.

Blue Hawaiian

Boozy Watermelon Slushy

On a hot summer day, there are few drinks as refreshing as this one! It's easy to customise to taste by swapping vodka for rum or more juice for a non-alcoholic serving.

Ingredients
2 cups frozen watermelon chunks
60ml vodka
30ml triple sec
30ml fresh lime juice
15ml simple syrup (optional)
Crushed ice
Lime slices and mint leaves

Method
● In a blender, combine the frozen watermelon chunks, vodka, triple sec, lime juice, and simple syrup.
● Blend until smooth.
● Add ice for a slushier consistency, if desired.
● Pour into glasses.
● Garnish with lime slices and mint leaves.

Long Island Iced Tea

Ingredients
15ml vodka
15ml white rum
15ml gin
15ml silver tequila
15ml triple sec
25ml fresh lemon juice
25ml simple syrup
Cola
Ice cubes
Mint leaves and lime wedges

Method
● Fill a shaker with ice.
● Add the vodka, rum, gin, tequila, triple sec, lemon juice, and simple syrup.
● Shake well and strain into a glass filled with ice.
● Top up with cola.
● Garnish with a sprig of mint and lime wedge.

Given the combination of strong spirits, Long Island Iced Tea is renowned for its alcoholic kick. We advise consuming this cocktail in moderation!

BUYER Barware

With these essentials, you'll be well-equipped to craft a wide range of delicious cocktails from the comfort of your home bar. Cheers to your mixology adventures!

Glassware Collection

DOUBLE OLD FASHIONED GLASS

The size of a double old-fashioned glass allows for serving drinks with large ice cubes or plenty of mixer, making it ideal for drinks like Old Fashioned cocktails, whisky on the rocks or rum and Coke.

CURVED ROCKS GLASS

A curved rocks glass is a short and stout glass with a rounded shape that is commonly used for serving spirits on the rocks or cocktails without ice. Perfect for getting to grips with a fancy spirit!

COLLINS GLASS

A Collins glass is a tall, narrow glass typically used for serving a variety of mixed drinks, especially those served over ice. This type of glass is named after the popular Tom Collins cocktail.

COUPE GLASS

Also known as a Champagne coupe, this is a glass with a broad, shallow bowl that is used for serving cocktails, particularly those that are shaken or stirred and strained, such as Martinis and Daiquiris.

MARTINI GLASS

Martinis originally came in smaller cocktail glasses but as the serving sizes grew in the '90s, the glass evolved into a larger, more conical shape with a longer stem and a wider rim.

HURRICANE GLASS

This tall, curvy glass is often used for tropical cocktails. It typically holds around 140ml of liquid and features a wide bowl that narrows at the top. Functional but also elegant.

Bartender Tool Kit

BAR SPOON

The extra-long and narrow handle of a bar spoon allows for easy reach into tall glasses or pitchers, while its twisted handle assists in smoothly stirring and layering ingredients without disturbing the cocktail's delicate balance.

BOSTON SHAKER

You'll need one of these if you want to feel like a real bartender. The fundamental tool consists of two parts, ensuring that the clean-up is simple. Use the larger part to mix your ingredients and then employ the smaller half at an angle, push in, hold and give it a good shake!

HAWTHORNE STRAINER

The Hawthorne strainer has been around since the late 1800s and is a vital tool in cocktail making. It's designed to fit snugly over a mixing glass or shaker tin to strain out ice and other solid ingredients from your drink as you pour it into the serving glass. The Hawthorne strainer ensures a clean and consistent pour, resulting in perfectly strained cocktails.

100 ULTIMATE COCKTAILS

You've already got at least one essential in your possession with this cocktail bookazine. We expect the 100 recipes will take you some time to get through while putting your mixing skills to the test!

WOODEN MUDDLER

A wooden muddler is a classic tool used to muddle fruits, herbs, and sugars in cocktails to extract their flavours and aromas. The textured end of the muddler helps release essential oils and juices, enhancing the taste and fragrance of the cocktail. With its natural appeal and functional design, a wooden muddler will add a rustic charm to your mixologist toolkit.

JIGGER

To achieve the perfect balance in any cocktail, it's imperative to master the art of the perfect measurement. The humble jigger is the best tool for achieving this. Typically made of stainless steel or other metal, a jigger has two cone-shaped cups on either end – one larger and one smaller – allowing bartenders to measure different volumes accurately.

41

During the '60s crème de violette was no longer being produced and the recipe was changed to include triple sec instead. In recent years, with crème de violette back in production, the original recipe has returned.

Aviation

Ingredients

50ml gin
10ml Maraschino liqueur
10ml crème de violette
20ml lemon juice
Maraschino cherry and lemon slice
Ice

Method

○ Fill a cocktail shaker with ice.
○ Add the gin, Maraschino liqueur, crème de violette, and lemon juice to the shaker.
○ Shake well until chilled.
○ Strain the mixture into a chilled cocktail glass.
○ Garnish with the Maraschino cherry and lemon slice

WE HAVE LIFT OFF

● The Aviation cocktail is a classic cocktail known for its elegant appearance and timeless flavour profile. This cocktail, with its pale purple hue and citrusy notes, is a perfect balance of botanical gin, floral crème de violette and zesty lemon juice. The addition of Maraschino liqueur adds depth and sweetness to this well-loved drink.

● Originating in the early 20th century, the Aviation has stood the test of time as a beloved cocktail for gin enthusiasts and cocktail connoisseurs alike. Its name is said to reflect its sky-blue colour, reminiscent of a cloudless sky.

● The Aviation cocktail continues to soar in popularity, captivating drinkers with its sophisticated taste and aesthetic appeal.

Paper Plane

The Paper Plane was created in 2008 by Sam Ross and Sasha Petraska with the name inspired by the M.I.A. track *Paper Planes*, a song often listened to while the drink was being created.

Ingredients
20ml bourbon
20ml Aperol
20ml Amaro Nonino
20ml freshly squeezed lemon juice
Ice

Method
● Fill a cocktail shaker with ice.
● Add the bourbon, Aperol, Amaro Nonino and lemon juice to the shaker.
● Shake well until chilled.
● Strain the mixture into a chilled cocktail glass.

Bramble

The Bramble takes its name from the bush on which the sweet blackberries that provide the principal flavour of the cocktail grow.

Ingredients

50ml gin
25ml freshly squeezed lemon juice
15ml sugar syrup
15ml crème de mûre
Fresh blackberries
Mint leaves
Crushed ice

Method

● Fill a rocks glass with crushed ice.
● In a cocktail shaker, combine the gin, lemon juice and sugar syrup.
● Fill the shaker with ice and shake well.
● Strain the mixture over the crushed ice in the glass.
● Drizzle the crème de mûre over the top.
● Garnish with blackberries and mint leaves.

Penicillin

The drink's name references the antibiotic Penicillin and is thought to convey health benefits. However, we don't recommend downing a few to cure any ailments!

Ingredients
60ml blended Scotch whisky
20ml fresh lemon juice
20ml honey syrup (10ml honey, 10ml water)
10ml ginger syrup
Islay single malt Scotch whisky
Candied ginger
Ice

Method
● In a shaker, combine the blended Scotch whisky, fresh lemon juice, honey syrup, and ginger syrup.
● Fill the shaker with ice and shake well. Strain the mixture into a rocks glass filled with ice.
● Float a small amount of Islay single malt Scotch whisky on top.
● Garnish with candied ginger.
● Stir gently and serve

Southside

This cocktail was apparently very popular with Al Capone and his associates who christened it Southside, after the South Side area in Chicago they dominated.

Ingredients
50ml gin
25ml lemon juice
15ml sugar syrup
Fresh mint leaves
Lime slice
Ice

Method
● In a shaker, muddle a few fresh mint leaves.
● Add gin, lemon juice, sugar syrup and ice cubes to the shaker.
● Shake well until chilled.
● Strain the mixture into a chilled cocktail glass.
● Garnish with a lime slice.

Ingredients
50ml gin
20ml freshly squeezed lemon juice
15ml raspberry syrup
1 egg white
Fresh raspberries
Ice cubes

Method
● Dry shake the egg white in a cocktail shaker for about 15 seconds.
● Add the gin, lemon juice, raspberry syrup, and ice cubes to the shaker.
● Shake well until chilled.
● Strain the mixture into a chilled cocktail glass.
● Garnish with fresh raspberries.

A key ingredient in the Clover Club cocktail is the addition of an egg white. When shaken forcefully, it creates a frothy texture that adds to the overall appeal of the drink.

Clover Club

Dark 'n' Stormy

Ingredients

60ml dark rum
120ml ginger beer
15ml freshly squeezed
lime juice
Lime wedge
Ice cubes

Method

- Fill a highball glass with ice cubes.
- Pour the dark rum over the ice.
- Squeeze the lime juice into the glass.
- Top up with ginger beer and stir gently to mix.
- Garnish with a lime wedge.

This cocktail is a close cousin to the Moscow Mule (see pg15) and should be an easy transition for vodka drinkers who would like to try something new, but not too different.

Corpse Reviver #2

Ingredients
25ml gin
25ml Cointreau
(orange liqueur)
25ml Lillet Blanc (or
Cocchi Americano)
25ml freshly squeezed
lemon juice
Absinthe
Orange twist
Ice cubes

Method
● Fill a shaker with ice cubes.
● Add the gin, Cointreau, Lillet Blanc, and lemon juice to the shaker.
● Shake well until chilled.
● Rinse a chilled cocktail glass with absinthe.
● Strain the mixture into the prepared glass.
● Garnish with an orange twist.

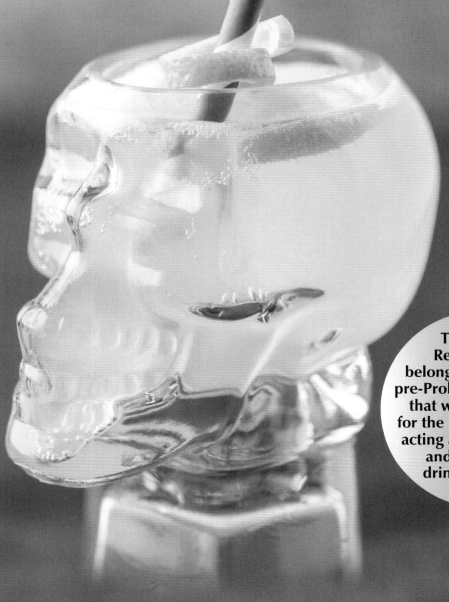

The Corpse Reviver No. 2 belongs to a family of pre-Prohibition cocktails that were consumed for the main purpose of acting as a pick-me-up and rousing the drinker from the dead!

Gold Rush

Not too dissimilar to a Whisky Sour (pg14), the Gold Rush instead uses honey syrup to deliver a richer and sweeter taste.

Ingredients
50ml bourbon
20ml honey syrup
(10ml honey, 10ml water)
25ml freshly squeezed
lemon juice
Lemon slice
Cocktail cherry
Ice cubes

Method
● Fill a cocktail shaker with ice.
● Add the bourbon, honey syrup, and lemon juice to the shaker.
● Shake well then strain into a rocks glass filled with ice.
● Garnish with a lemon slice and cocktail cherry.

Last Word

Asked to describe this drink to *The Washington Post*, Phil Ward, a former bartender at New York City's Pegu Club said, "A four-way car crash in which no one is hurt, and everyone's glad they met afterward." We've not read or heard a better description!

Ingredients
20ml gin
20ml green Chartreuse
20ml Maraschino liqueur
20ml freshly squeezed
lime juice
Lime twist
Ice cubes

Method
● Fill a cocktail shaker with ice.
● Add the gin, green Chartreuse, Maraschino liqueur and lime juice to the shaker.
● Shake well until chilled.
● Strain the mixture into a chilled cocktail glass.
● Garnish with a lime twist.

Smoky Martini

Ingredients

50ml gin
10ml dry vermouth
10ml Islay single malt
Scotch whisky
Lime slice
Ice cubes

Method

- Fill a mixing glass with ice cubes.
- Add the gin and dry vermouth to the mixing glass.
- Stir well until chilled.
- Strain the mixture into a chilled martini glass.
- Float the Islay single malt Scotch whisky on top.
- Garnish with a lime slice.

An easy variation on a Martini (pg8), the Smoky Martini has no vermouth and instead uses a dash of Scotch to back up the gin.

TEQUILA Mockingbird

A witty concoction of tequila, lime and sass. This drink is a literary delight for your taste buds.

Punny Cocktails!

Want to add a twist of humour to your dinner party drinks menu? Then look no further…

GRAPE Expectations

This cocktail promises a burst of grape flavoured vodka with a hint of floral notes, exceeding all flavour expectations. Just mix vodka, orange liqueur and grape juice.

GIN And Bear It

A classic gin and tonic with a playful name for those guests visiting after a tough week!

ABSINTHE Minded

A playful take on the powerful spirit for those who like to forget. Mix whisky, absinthe and bitters.

RUM
Forrest
RUM

Dive into the depths of this tropical concoction made with rum, pineapple, and a hint of coconut – it's a breathless adventure!

BOURBON
Voyage

Embark on a flavourful journey with a bourbon-based mixture that will transport your taste buds to new horizons. Make an Old Fashioned (pg9) or Mint Julep (pg18).

MINT Condition

Stay in mint condition with this refreshing blend of mint, vodka, and a splash of lime – the perfect remedy for any day.

BERRY-Go-Round

Take a spin with this berry-infused cocktail that's like a merry-go-round of fruity goodness – a delightful whirlwind for your palate. Try a Clover Club (pg47).

WHISKY
Business

Get down to "whisky" business with this bold blend of whisky, bitters, and a touch of sweetness – it means serious business!

SAKE
It Off

Shake it up with this sake-infused cocktail that might end up making you dance like nobody's watching! Just add Sake to a basic Margarita (pg10).

FIZZICAL
Attraction

Offering a light, airy texture with a refreshing citrus and floral profile, this drink attracts attention with its fizzy charm. Make a Paloma (pg25).

Spicy
Margarita

One of the great things about a Spicy Margarita is that it can be customised to suit individual tastes. If you prefer a milder drink, simply reduce the amount of chilli used. On the other hand, if you love the heat, feel free to up the spice!

IT'S GETTING HOT IN HERE

● Delving into the realm of bold flavours, the Spicy Margarita cocktail offers a tantalising twist on a favourite. This fiery concoction combines the tangy freshness of lime juice and the smooth warmth of tequila. The spicy kick from the jalapeños or hot sauce is the perfect finishing touch.

● The marriage of sweet agave syrup and spicy elements creates a harmonious blend that dances on the taste buds. Thanks to the spicy-salty flavours on the rim of the glass, each sip delivers a symphony of flavours that awaken the senses.

● The Spicy Margarita's contrasting flavours will appeal to those who crave a tipple with an adventurous edge. Whether enjoyed on a warm summer evening or as a fiery companion to Mexican cuisine, this sweet but spicy drink is a sure crowd-pleaser for those who enjoy a drink with a difference.

Ingredients

50ml tequila
25ml freshly squeezed lime juice
15ml agave syrup
1-2 slices of jalapeño or a dash of hot sauce
Salt and chilli powder
Pineapple wedge
Ice cubes

Method

● Rim a rocks glass with a mixture of salt and chilli powder.
● Fill the glass with ice.
● In a shaker, muddle the jalapeño slices (or add hot sauce), lime juice, and agave syrup.
● Add the tequila and ice to the shaker.
● Shake well to infuse the flavours.
● Strain the mixture into the prepared glass.
● Garnish with a pineapple wedge and a few slices of jalapeño.

Hemingway Daiquiri

Ingredients
50ml white rum
15ml Maraschino liqueur
25ml freshly squeezed grapefruit juice
15ml freshly squeezed lime juice
Grapefruit twist
Ice cubes

Method
● Fill a cocktail shaker with ice.
● Add the white rum, Maraschino liqueur, grapefruit juice, and lime juice to the shaker.
● Shake well until chilled.
● Strain the mixture into a chilled cocktail glass filled with ice.
● Garnish with a grapefruit twist.

Ernest Hemingway himself is reputed to have said about his favourite drink, "It shouldn't taste of rum, it shouldn't taste of lime and it shouldn't taste of sugar. It should just taste of daiquiri."

Strawberry Daiquiri

Ingredients

50ml white rum
25ml fresh lime juice
10ml sugar syrup
2 fresh strawberries
(with extra for garnish)
Crushed ice

Method

● Add the strawberries to a blender and blend until smooth.
● In a cocktail shaker, muddle the blended strawberries.
● Add the white rum, fresh lime juice, sugar syrup, and ice to the shaker.
● Shake well until chilled.
● Strain the mixture into a chilled cocktail glass.
● Garnish with a strawberry on the rim.

By mixing up the ingredients, lowering the sugar a little and adding strawberry puree this recipe produces a fruity twist on the classic Daiquiri (pg13).

Cucumber Collins

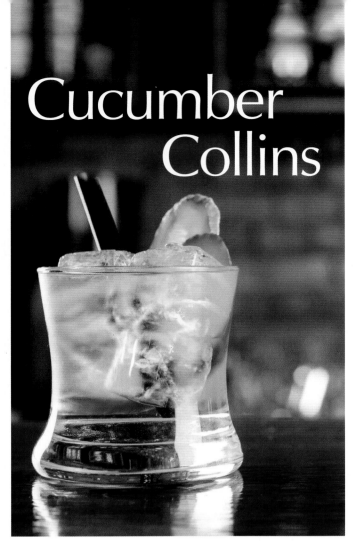

Cucumbers are rich in vitamins and minerals, low in calories and have a high water content to help keep your body hydrated.

Ingredients
50ml gin
25ml fresh lemon juice
15ml sugar syrup
4 slices of cucumber
Soda water
Ice cubes

Method
● In a cocktail shaker, muddle the cucumber slices.
● Add the gin, fresh lemon juice, and sugar syrup to the shaker.
● Fill the shaker with ice and shake well.
● Strain the mixture into a glass filled with ice.
● Top up with soda water.
● Garnish with a cucumber slice.

The Blueberry Spritzer

Traditionally, spritzers are made with wine. While this recipe suggests vodka, switching for white wine would ensure a different but equally refreshing taste.

Ingredients
50ml blueberry vodka
25ml fresh lime juice
15ml simple syrup
Blueberries
Mint leaves
Soda water
Ice cubes

Method
● In a glass, muddle a few blueberries and mint leaves.
● Add the blueberry vodka, fresh lime juice, and simple syrup to the glass.
● Fill the glass with ice.
● Top up with soda water.
● Stir gently to mix the ingredients.
● Garnish with a few blueberries and a mint leaf.

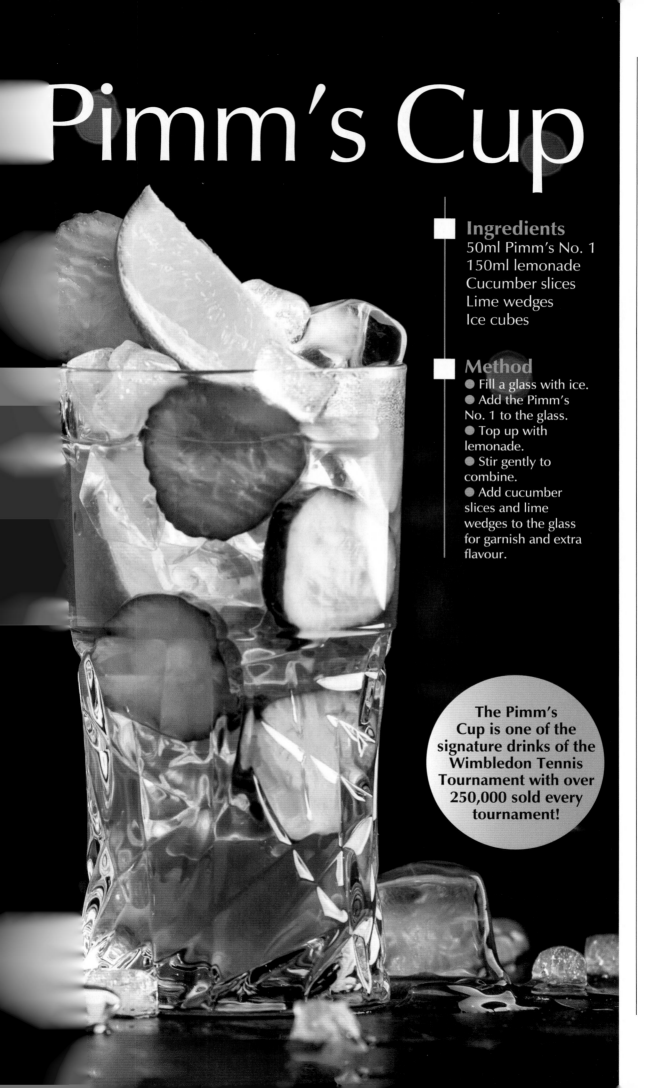

Pimm's Cup

Ingredients
50ml Pimm's No. 1
150ml lemonade
Cucumber slices
Lime wedges
Ice cubes

Method
● Fill a glass with ice.
● Add the Pimm's No. 1 to the glass.
● Top up with lemonade.
● Stir gently to combine.
● Add cucumber slices and lime wedges to the glass for garnish and extra flavour.

The Pimm's Cup is one of the signature drinks of the Wimbledon Tennis Tournament with over 250,000 sold every tournament!

El Diablo

Ingredients
50ml tequila
25ml fresh lime juice
10ml crème de cassis
Ginger beer
Orange wedge
Ice cubes

Method
● Fill a glass with ice.
● Add the tequila, fresh lime juice, and crème de cassis to the glass.
● Stir gently to mix the ingredients.
● Top up with ginger beer.
● Garnish with an orange wedge.
● Stir gently once more before serving.

This cocktail has become a popular choice for tequila lovers looking for a fruity and flavourful mixed drink.

Ingredients

50ml vodka
25ml triple sec
25ml fresh lemon juice
10ml simple syrup
Sugar (optional)
Lemon twist
Ice cubes

Method

● Rim a Martini glass with sugar by running a lemon wedge around the edge and dipping it in sugar, if desired.
● In a shaker, combine the vodka, triple sec, fresh lemon juice, and simple syrup.
● Fill the shaker with ice and shake well.
● Strain the mixture into the prepared Martini glass.
● Garnish with a lemon twist.

The Lemon Drop is commonly mistaken for a Martini, yet it's essentially a Vodka Crusta, evolving from brandy-based sours. It blends sweet and tart flavours, for a timeless taste.

Lemon Drop Martini

Luxury Libations

From exquisite concoctions featuring rare vintage spirits to Martinis adorned with diamonds, these drinks epitomise opulence at its finest.

This Martini from Tokyo's Ritz-Carlton stands out as one of the most extravagant cocktails in the world, priced at over £17,000.

DIAMONDS ARE FOREVER MARTINI

This luxurious drink features a stunning diamond at the bottom of the glass, elevating the drinking experience to a whole new level of opulence. The cocktail itself is a classic Martini, made with premium vodka and a hint of vermouth, creating a sophisticated and timeless flavour profile. Story has it that only two have been sold to date. Perhaps the price tag is standing in the way of further sales!

ONO CHAMPAGNE COCKTAIL

The Ono Champagne Cocktail is a celebration in a glass, renowned as one of the most lavish and indulgent cocktails in the world. Priced at a staggering £8,000, this opulent creation features the finest ingredients, blending Charles Heidsieck Champagne Charlie 1981 and Rémy Martin Louis XIII Black Pearl cognac. The cocktail is then finished with an edible, 18-karat gold leaf. Served at the Encore Wynn Las Vegas, the Ono Champagne Cocktail is not just a drink but a statement of extravagance and sophistication.

MARTINI ON THE ROCK

The Martini On The Rock cocktail is a drink that epitomises elegance and luxury, offering a unique and extravagant twist on the classic Martini. Priced at £8,000, this cocktail stands out for its presentation – a diamond at the bottom of the glass. This exquisite drink is made with premium gin or vodka, vermouth, and is served chilled. However, best to plan ahead as it requires a three-day advance reservation and an appointment with a jewellery maker!

RITZ-PARIS SIDECAR

The Sidecar cocktail was created at the legendary Ritz Hotel in Paris, so it's no surprise that this hotel also claims the most expensive Sidecar in the world, and one of the most expensive drinks in the world. Served in a chilled glass with a sugared rim, this exquisite drink is made with Cognac bottled between 1830 and 1870.

L'IMPERIAL

Visit the Baccarat Hotel in New York City and you'll find the L'Imperial Cocktail. A true embodiment of luxury and sophistication, offering a unique and opulent drinking experience. Coming in at the princely sum £4,000, this exquisite cocktail combines the finest ingredients. It should be said that the crystal glass it is served in is valued at £3,000 and it is yours to take away as a souvenir. A forever memento of that time you spent £4,000 on one cocktail!

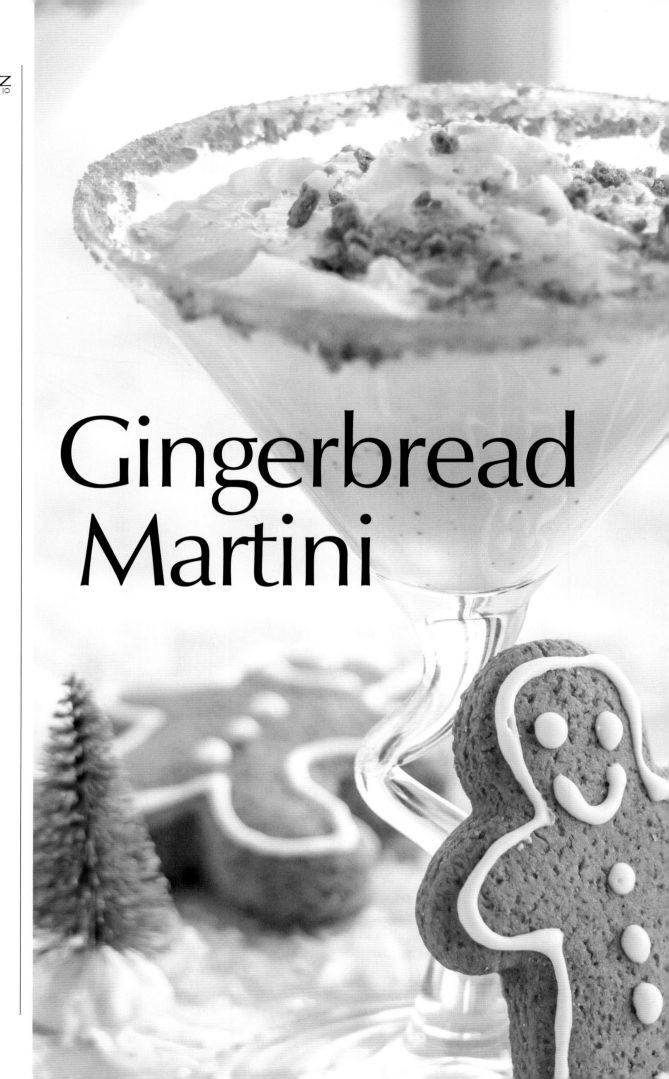

Gingerbread Martini

You can take the creaminess of this one up a notch further and including some vanilla ice cream in your shaker to create an extra special foamy top layer!

Ingredients

50ml spiced rum
25ml ginger liqueur
25ml Irish cream liqueur
25ml milk or cream
Gingerbread syrup
Cinnamon sugar
Ice cubes

Method

● Rim a Martini glass with gingerbread syrup and dip it in cinnamon sugar.
● In a shaker, combine the spiced rum, ginger liqueur, Irish cream liqueur, and milk or cream.
● Add a dash of gingerbread syrup to the shaker.
● Fill the shaker with ice and shake well.
● Strain the mixture into the prepared Martini glass.
● Sprinkle some ground cinnamon on top for garnish.

'TIS THE SEASON

● Step into the festive spirit with a Gingerbread Martini. The perfect winter drink, it captures all the warmth and sweetness of the season in a glass. Blending the rich flavours of spiced rum, ginger liqueur and Irish cream with a hint of gingerbread syrup, this is luxurious drink perfect for festive gatherings or cosy nights by the fire.

● An instant crowdpleaser, this delicious cocktail's warming flavours and creamy texture make for smooth sipping. Just the right mix of sweet from the Irish cream and spicy from the rum and ginger, it is a perfect after dinner treat at a Christmas get together with family or friends.

● Sink into a comfortable couch with a delicious Gingerbread Martini and let its festive flavours transport you to a winter wonderland. Embrace the excesses of the season with this indulgent treat that promises to envelop you in the spirit of celebration and merriment to the very last last drop. Happy holidays!

Pumpkin Spice Martini

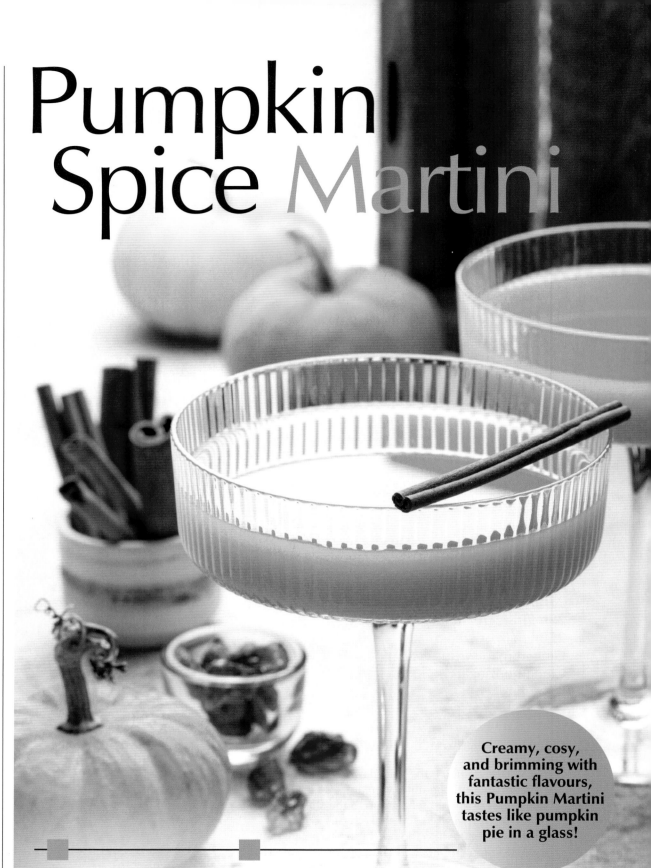

Creamy, cosy, and brimming with fantastic flavours, this Pumpkin Martini tastes like pumpkin pie in a glass!

Ingredients
50ml spiced rum
25ml pumpkin puree
25ml maple syrup
25ml cream or milk
Pumpkin pie spice
Cinnamon stick
Ice cubes

Method
● In a shaker, combine the spiced rum, pumpkin puree, maple syrup, and cream or milk.
● Add a pinch of pumpkin pie spice to the shaker.
● Fill the shaker with ice and shake well.
● Strain the mixture into a glass filled with ice.
● Garnish with a cinnamon stick.

Cranberry Mule

Ingredients
50ml vodka
25ml cranberry juice
15ml fresh lime juice
Ginger beer
Fresh cranberries
Lime wedges
Ice cubes

Method
● Fill a copper mug or glass with ice.
● Add the vodka, cranberry juice, and fresh lime juice to the glass.
● Top up with ginger beer.
● Stir gently to mix the ingredients.
● Garnish with fresh cranberries and a lime wedge.

If you can't get enough of cranberries, then this cocktail is definitely one for you to enjoy while sitting watching your favourite Christmas film.

Pomegranate Champagne

Pomegranates are low in calories and fat yet high in fibre, making them a healthy choice for any menu.

Ingredients

50ml pomegranate juice
10ml orange liqueur (such as Cointreau)
Chilled Champagne or sparkling wine
Pomegranate seeds
Rosemary sprig

Method

● In a Champagne flute, pour the pomegranate juice and orange liqueur.
● Top up the glass with chilled Champagne or sparkling wine.
● Gently stir to combine.
● Garnish with pomegranate seeds and the rosemary sprig.

Spiced Apple Cider

If you prefer a sweeter cocktail, you can try adding 10ml of maple syrup to this recipe and mix with other ingredients in the glass at the outset.

Ingredients

50ml spiced rum
100ml apple cider
15ml lemon juice
Cinnamon stick
Apple slices
Thyme sprig
Brown sugar

Method

● Rim the glass with brown sugar then pour in the spiced rum, apple cider and lemon juice. Stir well.
● Fill the glass with ice.
● Garnish with a cinnamon stick, thyme sprig and apple slices.

No flavour says Christmas quite like peppermint. This Candy Cane Martini is a perfect balance of fabulous flavour and a visual treat to match!

Ingredients
50ml vanilla vodka
25ml peppermint schnapps
25ml white chocolate liqueur
Splash of grenadine
Small candy cane
Coconut flakes
Ice cube

Method
● Coat the rim of a Martini glass with coconut flakes.
● In a shaker, combine the vanilla vodka, peppermint schnapps, white chocolate liqueur, and a splash of grenadine.
● Fill the shaker with ice and shake well.
● Strain the mixture into the prepared Martini glass.
● Garnish with a candy cane.

Pink Candy Cane Martini

Wassail

Another option for this cocktail is to substitute the cider and dry white wine for brown ale and Oloroso sherry.

Ingredients
750ml apple cider
250ml dry white wine
100ml brandy
100g brown sugar
Cinnamon sticks
1 orange, sliced
1 apple, sliced
Cloves

Method
● In a large pot, combine the apple cider, dry white wine, brandy, brown sugar, two cinnamon sticks, orange slices, and apple slices.
● Heat the mixture over low heat, stirring to dissolve the sugar. Simmer gently for about 20-30 minutes to allow the flavours to meld.
● Ladle the Wassail into mugs.
● Garnish with whole cloves and a cinnamon stick.

Mulled Wine

Ingredients

750ml red wine
75g caster sugar
60ml brandy (optional)
1 cinnamon stick
4 cloves
2 star anise
100ml cranberry juice
1 orange peel
Sprig of rosemary

Method

● In a saucepan, combine the red wine, caster sugar, cinnamon stick, cloves, star anise, and orange peel.
● Heat the mixture over low heat, stirring until the sugar dissolves. Simmer gently for about 15 minutes.
● Stir in the cranberry juice and continue to heat until warm.
● Strain the mixture into mugs or heatproof glasses.
● Garnish with an orange twist and a sprig of rosemary.

You can also prepare mulled wine in a slow cooker, allowing it to simmer on the low setting for 1-2 hours before serving. Adjust the sweetness and spices according to your taste preferences.

Eggnog Martini

Experiment with different types of flavoured vodka or liqueurs to customise the cocktail to your liking.

Ingredients
50ml eggnog
50ml raspberry vodka
25ml amaretto
Ground nutmeg
Brown sugar
Ice

Method
● Rim a Martini glass with brown sugar.
● In a shaker, combine the eggnog, raspberry vodka and amaretto. Fill the shaker with ice and shake well.
● Strain the mixture into the Martini glass
● Dust the top with nutmeg.

Hot Toddy

A Hot Toddy is the ultimate hot drink! With origins dating back to the mid-18th century, this is a drink often consumed by those who are feeling sick to try and rid them of a cold or sore throat.

Ingredients
50ml whisky
1tbsp honey
25ml fresh lemon juice
Hot water
Rosemary sprig
Lemon slice

Method
● In a heatproof glass, combine the whisky, honey and fresh lemon juice.
● Add hot water to the glass and stir until the honey dissolves.
● Garnish with the rosemary sprig and lemon slice.
● Stir gently to infuse the flavours.

Christmas Punch

Ingredients

750ml cranberry juice
500ml orange juice
1l lemonade
60ml simple syrup
100ml grenadine
Fresh cranberries
Lime wedges
Rosemary sprigs
Ice cubes

Method

● In a punch bowl, combine the cranberry juice, simple syrup, orange juice and lemonade.
● Stir in the grenadine for sweetness and colour.
● Add fresh cranberries, lime wedges and rosemary sprigs for decoration.
● Fill the bowl with ice to keep the punch cold. Stir well and serve.

The ultimate festive tipple, a festive punch will taste different depending on whose party you're at! Experiment with added some fresh ginger, grated nutmeg or a pinch of allspice. Add sparkling wine or rum for an alcoholic version, if desired.

Irish Coffee

Ingredients
50ml Irish whiskey
100ml hot coffee
2tsp brown sugar
50ml double cream

Method
● Heat a heatproof glass by rinsing it out with boiling water.
● Add the brown sugar to the glass.
● Pour in the hot coffee and stir until the sugar dissolves.
● Add the Irish whiskey and stir to combine.
● Gently whip the double cream until slightly thickened but still pourable.
● Pour the cream over the back of a spoon to float it on top of the coffee.

The Irish Coffee may not be the first coffee drink with alcohol but it has certainly gone on to become one of the most famous. A drink that can wake you up in the morning or keep you going at night!

Hot Buttered Rum

It's hot, it has butter, and it has rum! Hot Buttered Rum is quite simply comfort food in a mug.

Ingredients

50ml dark rum
1tbsp unsalted butter
1tbsp brown sugar
Pinch of ground cinnamon
Pinch of ground nutmeg
Pinch of ground cloves
Boiling water
Cinnamon stick

Method

● In a heatproof glass, cream together the unsalted butter, brown sugar and spices.
● Add the dark rum to the glass and stir to combine.
● Fill the glass with boiling water and stir until well mixed.
● Garnish with a cinnamon stick.

The key is using the highest-quality ingredients possible with your crème de cacao and chocolate liqueur.

Chocolate Martini

Ingredients

50ml vodka
25ml chocolate liqueur
25ml crème de cacao
25ml cream or milk
Chocolate shavings
Ice

Method

● Rim a Martini glass with chocolate shavings.
● In a shaker, combine the vodka, chocolate liqueur, crème de cacao, and cream or milk.
● Fill the shaker with ice and shake well.
● Strain the mixture into the prepared Martini glass.
● Garnish with a sprinkle of chocolate shavings on top.

SWEETEN YOUR DAY

● Indulge in the velvety sophistication of a Chocolate Martini, a luxurious cocktail that combines the rich flavours of vodka, chocolate liqueur, crème de cacao, and cream.

● This decadent drink tantalises the taste buds with its creamy texture and luscious cocoa notes, making it a favourite among cocktail enthusiasts and sweet-toothed connoisseurs alike.

● The Chocolate Martini is a timeless classic that brings a touch of elegance to any occasion, whether sipped at a glamorous evening soiree or enjoyed as a delightful after-dinner treat. With its indulgent blend of ingredients and smooth finish, this cocktail is a perfect balance of sophistication and sweetness, creating a truly irresistible drinking experience.

Banana Daiquiri

The Banana Daiquiri dates back to the early 20th century when it was first created in Cuba. This delightful cocktail has since grown in popularity thanks to its refreshing taste and smooth texture.

Ingredients

50ml white rum
1 ripe banana
25ml fresh lime juice
15ml simple syrup
Banana slice
Ice

Method

● In a blender, combine the white rum, ripe banana, fresh lime juice and simple syrup.
● Add a cup of ice to the blender.
● Blend until smooth and creamy.
● Pour the mixture into a chilled glass. Garnish with a banana slice.

Ingredients
25ml crème de menthe
25ml crème de cacao
25ml double cream
Mint leaf
Ice

Method
- Fill a shaker with ice.
- Add the crème de menthe, crème de cacao, and double cream to the shaker.
- Shake well until chilled.
- Strain the mixture into a chilled glass.
- Garnish with a mint leaf.

The sugary punch of a Grasshopper cocktail means it can be a great drink of choice for those who are looking for something that doesn't have a super-strong taste of alcohol.

Grasshopper

Brandy Alexander

The Brandy Alexander tastes like a milkshake with a light alcohol taste. It's most commonly served in a Martini glass, which adds to the elegance to its appearance.

Ingredients
50ml brandy
25ml dark crème de cacao
25ml cream
Nutmeg
Ice

Method
● Fill a shaker with ice.
● Add the brandy, dark crème de cacao, and cream to the shaker.
● Shake well until chilled.
● Strain the mixture into a chilled glass.
● Garnish with a sprinkle of nutmeg on top.

White Russian

The White Russian was first served in the '60s when someone added cream to the Black Russian. Neither drink is Russian in origin but is linked via the use of vodka.

Ingredients
50ml vodka
25ml coffee liqueur (eg Kahlúa)
25ml cream
Ice

Method
● Fill a glass with ice.
● Add the vodka and coffee liqueur to the glass.
● Stir gently to mix.
● Pour the cream over the back of a spoon to float it on top of the mixture.

Whisky Mac Coffee Cups are a popular choice for those who appreciate complex and comforting cocktails with a modern twist.

Whisky Mac Coffee Cups

Ingredients (makes 4)

5 sheets leaf gelatine
400ml freshly brewed hot coffee
3tbsp caster sugar
75ml Scotch whisky
50ml ginger wine
150ml single cream
Chocolate coffee beans and festive sprinkles

Method

● Soak 4 sheets gelatine in cold water for 5 minutes.
● Drain well and add to the hot coffee along with the sugar; stir until dissolved.
● Stir in the whisky and ginger wine. Leave to cool.
● Pour into 4 x 150ml cups, leaving at least a 1cm gap at the top of each. Chill for 2hrs or until set.
● Soak and drain the remaining gelatine as above.
● Heat the cream until hot but not boiling. Stir in the gelatine until dissolved.
● Leave to cool then pour a layer on top of each jelly. Chill for 1hr. Garnish with the beans and sprinkles.

Margarita & Tacos

The zesty flavours of a Margarita (pg10) complement the spices in tacos. A Mojito or Bloody Mary can also be natural partners to other dishes with a spicy kick.

Taste Bud
Tango

It's raining cocktails!

Pairing cocktails with food can enhance the overall dining experience. If you are wondering where to start, here are some interesting cocktail and food pairings to kick things off…

Negroni & Charcuterie

The bitterness of a Negroni (pg12) pairs well with the richness of cured meats and cheeses. Consider also with pasta dishes or stuffed porchetta.

Sangria & Tapas

A variety of pairings work well with Spanish tapas dishes, but the fruity notes of Sangria should keep it at the top of your list. Olé!

G&T & Seafood

The crispness of a Gin & Tonic is a great match for the lightness of seafood. Gin also makes an excellent palate cleanser when sitting down to enjoy a dish with strong flavours.

Old Fashioned & Barbecue

The richness of bourbon, alongside the sweet elements of the cocktail, complements the smoky sweetness of barbecue meats really well.

Paloma & Mexican

The citrus flavours of a Paloma (p25) go well with traditional Mexican cuisine. The acidity of the grapefruit juice cuts through the heat of any dish, resulting in a refreshing balance.

Mojito & Ceviche

The minty freshness of a Mojito (pg11) is a perfect match for the citrusy flavours of ceviche. Fish curries, smoked salmon or crispy squid can also work as a pairing.

76

FOR THE ADVENTUROUS

Ingredients
50ml bourbon
25ml sweet vermouth
25ml Campari
Orange slice
Ice

Method
● Fill a mixing glass with ice.
● Add the bourbon, sweet vermouth, and Campari to the mixing glass.
● Stir well to combine and chill the mixture.
● Strain the mixture into a glass filled with ice.
● Garnish with an orange slice.

If you're a fan of the classic Italian Negroni cocktail (pg12), then the Boulevardier is one you really should try.

Boulevardier

CLASS IN A GLASS

● Step into the world of refined libations with the Boulevardier cocktail, a blend of bourbon, sweet vermouth, and Campari that embodies timeless elegance in a glass.

● Originating in the 1920s Parisian cocktail scene, this classic drink exudes an air of sophistication and charm, drawing in cocktail enthusiasts with its perfect balance of bold flavours and bitter undertones. The Boulevardier's allure lies in its complex profile, where the richness of bourbon meets the sweetness of vermouth and the bitterness of Campari, creating a harmonious symphony of tastes on the palate.

● Served over ice and garnished with an orange slice, this cocktail is a true masterpiece that transcends trends, offering a taste of timeless quality with every sip.

Mezcal Margarita

Ingredients

50ml mezcal
25ml Cointreau or triple sec
25ml fresh lime juice
Agave nectar or simple syrup
Lime wedge and mint leaves
Salt (optional)
Ice

Method

● Rim a glass with salt (optional).
● In a shaker, combine the mezcal, Cointreau or triple sec, fresh lime juice, and agave nectar or simple syrup.
● Fill the shaker with ice and shake well.
● Strain the mixture into the prepared glass filled with ice.
● Garnish with the lime wedge and mint leaves.

The Mezcal Margarita is a modern twist on the classic cocktail and is known for its smoky flavour. Made with mezcal, a spirit derived from the agave plant, it has a unique flavour that sets it apart from a classic Margarita.

Corpse Reviver #1

Ingredients
25ml brandy
25ml apple brandy
25ml sweet vermouth
Orange twist

Method
● Fill a mixing glass with ice.
● Add the brandy, apple brandy, and sweet vermouth to the mixing glass. Stir well.
● Strain the mixture into a chilled cocktail glass.
● Garnish with the orange twist.

The Corpse Reviver #1 is perhaps inappropriately named given it is likely to function best as a night cap as opposed to the Corpse Reviver #2 (pg49) which is more the "reviver".

FOR THE ADVENTUROUS

Oaxaca Old Fashioned

Ingredients
50ml mezcal
10ml agave nectar
1 dash Angostura bitters
1 dash orange bitters
Orange twist
Ice

Method
● In a mixing glass, add the agave nectar, Angostura bitters, and orange bitters.
● Stir to combine and dissolve the agave nectar.
● Add the mezcal and stir well.
● Fill a glass with ice.
● Strain the mixture over the ice in the glass.
● Express the oils of an orange twist over the drink and use as garnish.

This modern-day cocktail classic is one you won't regret trying. It's a sweet, smoky after-dinner drink that is a great way to follow a dinner party feast.

Jungle Bird

FOR THE ADVENTUROUS

Ingredients
50ml dark rum
75ml pineapple juice
15ml Campari
15ml simple syrup
25ml fresh lime juice
Pineapple leaves
Ice

Method
● Fill a shaker with ice.
● Add the dark rum, pineapple juice, Campari, simple syrup, and fresh lime juice to the shaker.
● Shake well to mix the ingredients.
● Strain the mixture into a glass filled with ice.
● Garnish with the pineapple leaves.

Created by Jeffrey Ong when he worked as beverage manager at the Kuala Lumpur Hilton hotel's Aviary Bar in the '70s, this welcome drink was named after the tropical birds kept in a netted area near the pool area which could be seen from the bar window.

Make mine a *treble*!

Multi-Sensory Experiences

■ **Sound Match**
Curate a playlist of music or choose a soundtrack that match the theme or flavour profile of the cocktails you serve.

■ **Aromatic Pairings**
Enhance the drinking experience with aromatherapy, using scented misters or essential oil infused coasters.

Interactive Cocktails

■ **DIY Flavour Drops**
Provide your guests with concentrated flavour drops (like sour, bitter or sweet) that they can add to their cocktails according to their taste preference.

■ **Colour Changing Drinks**
Utilise ingredients like butterfly pea flower or pH-sensitive syrups that change colour when mixed with acidic or alkaline ingredients.

Edible Interest

■ **Flower Ice Cubes**
Edible flowers frozen inside ice cubes add a striking floral touch to your cocktail as they melt.

■ **Sweet Garnishes**
Use sweets as garnish to add a playful element that complements the drink's flavour.

Innovate To Elevate

Exploring something fresh and unusual with the cocktails you serve can provide an amazing drinking experience that goes beyond taste, engaging all senses and perhaps even introducing an educational element. Check out these innovative ideas that can elevate cocktails from the ordinary to the extraordinary!

Make It A Sustainable Serve

■ Upcycled Ingredients
Use by-products from food preparation, like fruit peels or herb stems, to create infusions or garnishes.

■ Take A Zero-Waste Approach
Don't stock up on extra ingredients if you won't use them, and use those you do up instead of buying new.

Shake It Up

■ Savoury Swaps
Incorporate surprising savoury ingredients like bacon, cheese, or even small amounts of seafood to create a unique flavour profile – seaweed and salt create a coastal vibe!

■ Herbal and Medicinal Twists
Use adaptogens, CBD, or herbal supplements that offer health benefits or mood-enhancing properties.

Dimensional Drinks

■ Layer Up
Use liqueurs with different densities to create aesthetically appealing layered drinks.

■ Frozen Core Cocktails
Create a cocktail with a frozen core of a different, complementary flavour that slowly releases as it melts.

Tell A Tale

■ Story-Driven Menus
Serve guests a flight of cocktails to tell part of a story, with unique drinks which allow you to tell a story with every sip.

■ Cultural Journeys
Take yourself on a tipple-based tour of different countries or regions through locally inspired drinks!

Health-Conscious Options

■ Low-ABV & Non-Alcoholic Variants
Cocktails that are full of flavour but low in alcohol or completely non-alcoholic, are a sophisticated way to raise a glass without any of the side-effects the next day!

■ Superfood Cocktails
Incorporate superfoods like acai, goji berries or turmeric for their health benefits and vibrant colours.

Red Hook

Ingredients
60ml rye whiskey
15ml Punt e Mes (or sweet vermouth)
5ml Maraschino liqueur
Maraschino cherry
Ice

Method
● Fill a mixing glass with ice.
● Add the rye whiskey, Punt e Mes or sweet vermouth, and Maraschino liqueur to the mixing glass.
● Stir well to chill the mixture.
● Strain the cocktail into a chilled glass.
● Garnish with a Maraschino cherry.

The Red Hook cocktail was the first variation of the Manhattan (pg9) that took its name from the Brooklyn neighbourhood, creating a trend that saw the Bensonhurst and Greenpoint cocktails follow.

OFF THE HOOK

● The Red Hook cocktail is a classic libation that pays homage to the golden era of mixology. This refined drink is a blend of rye whiskey, Punt e Mes or sweet vermouth, and a touch of Maraschino liqueur, creating a harmonious balance of flavours and aromas.

● The Red Hook exudes an air of old-world charm with a modern twist, captivating cocktail enthusiasts with its smooth texture and complex profile.

● Served in a chilled glass and garnished with a Maraschino cherry, this cocktail is a true testament to the artistry and craftsmanship of the cocktail renaissance.

Vieux Carré

Ingredients
20ml rye whiskey
20ml cognac
20ml sweet vermouth
1tsp Benedictine
1 dash Angostura bitters
1 dash Peychaud's bitters
Lemon twist
Ice

Method
● Fill a mixing glass with ice.
● Add the rye whiskey, cognac, sweet vermouth, Benedictine, Angostura bitters, and Peychaud's bitters to the mixing glass.
● Stir well to incorporate all the ingredients.
● Strain the mixture into a chilled glass over ice.
● Express the oils of a lemon twist over the drink and use as garnish.

The cocktail is named after the French term for the "Old Square", which refers to the French Quarter in New Orleans, the city in which it was created.

Scofflaw

Ingredients
50ml rye whiskey
25ml dry vermouth
25ml fresh lemon juice
15ml grenadine
1 dash orange bitters
Lemon twist
Ice

Method
- Fill a shaker with ice.
- Add the rye whiskey, dry vermouth, fresh lemon juice, grenadine, and orange bitters to the shaker.
- Shake well to mix the ingredients.
- Strain the mixture into a glass filled with ice.
- Garnish with a lemon twist.

The term "Scofflaw" was popularised during the Prohibition as a way to describe people who flouted the ban on alcohol. The Scofflaw cocktail gained popularity as a symbol of rebellion against the restrictive laws of the time.

Naked And Famous

First created as recently as 2011, this modern cocktail gained popularity for its unique combination of equal parts mezcal, Yellow Chartreuse, Aperol, and lime juice, which results in a complex and well-balanced drink.

Ingredients
20ml mezcal
20ml Yellow Chartreuse
20ml Aperol
20ml lime juice
Ice

Method
● Fill a shaker with ice.
● Add the mezcal, Yellow Chartreuse, Aperol, and lime juice to the shaker.
● Shake well to combine the ingredients.
● Strain the mixture into a glass.

Twentieth Century

This classic cocktail is named after the luxurious Twentieth Century Limited train that operated between New York City and Chicago from 1902 to 1967.

Ingredients
40ml gin
20ml Lillet Blanc
20ml white crème de cacao
20ml lemon juice
Lemon twist
Ice

Method
● Fill a shaker with ice.
● Add the gin, Lillet Blanc, white crème de cacao, and lemon juice to the shaker.
● Shake well to mix the ingredients.
● Strain the mixture into a glass.
● Garnish with a lemon twist.

Rhubarb Margarita

Ingredients
60ml tequila
30ml fresh lime juice
30ml rhubarb syrup
15ml triple sec or Cointreau
Rhubarb twist
Salt (optional)
Ice cubes

Method
● To make the rhubarb syrup, combine chopped rhubarb, sugar, and water in a saucepan. Simmer over a low heat until the rhubarb is soft and the sugar has dissolved.
● Strain the mixture and let the syrup cool.
● Rim a glass with salt (optional) and fill it with ice cubes.
● In a shaker, combine tequila, fresh lime juice, rhubarb syrup, and triple sec/Cointreau.
● Add ice and shake well.
● Strain the mixture into the prepared glass.
● Garnish with a rhubarb twist.

The easy-to-make rhubarb syrup can be increased in volume and stored well in the fridge for a few weeks where it can then be used in other cocktail recipes or drizzled over ice cream or pancakes.

LET'S TWIST AGAIN

● Wondering what to do with all of that rhubarb that is growing in your garden? Then look no further than this tantalising Rhubarb Margarita.

● This tangy twist combines the bold flavours of tequila, fresh lime juice, and a homemade rhubarb syrup to create a harmonious balance of sweet and tangy notes. As you take a sip of this vibrant concoction, the tartness of the rhubarb syrup dances on your palate, complemented by the citrusy kick of lime and the smooth warmth of tequila.

● Garnished with a rhubarb twist, this cocktail is not just a treat for the taste buds but a feast for the eyes.

Pear Martini

The refreshing and fruity appeal of a Pear Martini makes it a versatile cocktail that pairs well with a host of appetisers such as cheese platters, seafood dishes including sushi, and even savoury bites like bruschetta.

Ingredients
50ml pear vodka
25ml elderflower liqueur
25ml pear juice
½ fresh lime juice
Ice cubes
Rosemary sprig

Method
● Fill a cocktail shaker with ice cubes.
● Add the pear vodka, elderflower liqueur, pear juice, and fresh lime juice to the shaker.
● Shake well until the mixture is thoroughly chilled.
● Strain the cocktail into a chilled Martini glass.
● Garnish with the rosemary sprig.

Chilli Chocolate Martini

Ingredients
50ml vodka
25ml chocolate liqueur
25ml chilli liqueur
Ice cubes
Lime and orange zest
Salt (optional)

Method
● Rim a Martini glass with salt.
● Fill a cocktail shaker with ice cubes.
● Add vodka, chocolate liqueur and chilli liqueur to the shaker.
● Shake well until the mixture is thoroughly chilled.
● Strain the cocktail into the Martini glass.
● Garnish with the lime and orange zest.

A twist on the Chocolate Martini (pg76), this version replaces the crème de cacao for chilli liqueur which adds some warmth you may love!

101

Lavender Lemonade

Ingredients
900ml cold water
6tbsp sugar
1tbsp dried lavender
200ml freshly squeezed lemon juice
60ml limoncello
60ml gin
Ice cubes
Lavender sprigs and lemon slices

Method
● To make the lavender syrup, combine 450ml of the water, sugar and dried lavender in a saucepan. Bring to a simmer over a medium heat, stirring until the sugar has dissolved.
● Remove from the heat and let it cool to room temperature.
● Strain the lavender syrup and discard the lavender.
● In a large pitcher, mix the freshly squeezed lemon juice, lavender syrup, limoncello, gin, ice cubes and the other 450ml of cold water.
● Pour into glasses and garnish with the lavender sprigs and lemon slices.

Lemonade and lavender is a classic combination. The floral tones of lavender work in sync with the sweet sharpness of citrus. This cocktail can work equally as well with gin or vodka.

The Sober Truth

Which hangover cures really work the morning after the mojito before? We put them to the test.

Gone are the days of stumbling home at sunrise, fresh-faced and ready to take on the world. Instead, we've reached a point where even the slightest sniff of our preferred spirit can leave us in the sorriest of states. Where everything hurts – from our heads to our egos – and the loom of an existential crisis is almost as inevitable as uttering that insincere promise of "never again". Fortunately, there is hope! In a mission to vanquish the fear that accompanies waking up in a tilt-a-whirl, with a mouth drier than a bottle of London's finest, we set out to find a real "cure" for the much-dreaded hangover. Here's what we found...

1 Let's Get Physical

CURE: Exercise **THEORY:** Sweating out toxins + releasing endorphins + easing 3am kebab guilt = happy hangover
VERDICT: The mere thought of going for a run with a hangover was almost as bad as the hangover itself, so we ditched the running shoes and opted for a less strenuous, non-vomit-inducing activity. Yoga. It really helped and, if nothing else, provided a welcome distraction from our suffering.

2 Greasy Does It

CURE: The fry-up **THEORY:** Carbs + bacon = life (and something about replenishing depleted sugars)
VERDICT: Cooking was an absolute chore. Standing over a hot pan, sweating profusely, was as dreadful as it sounds, but eating? Eating was worse. After feeling two-stone heavier, the lethargy really kicked in, followed swiftly by nausea and total, unadulterated regret.

3 Pickle Your Fancy

CURE: Pickle juice **THEORY:** Salt + vinegar + electrolytes = bye bye, headache
VERDICT: Pickle fans, rejoice. Everyone else, sorry, but this seems to actually work. After a good few glugs of acidic awfulness the hangover headache did subside. Of course, we won't be trying this again any time soon. No-one likes pickles that much.

4 Hair Of The Dog

CURE: More alcohol **THEORY:** GIN + GIN = WIN
VERDICT: Stomaching the smell was the first hurdle. Keeping it down was the second. Handling the shame of cracking open a bottle at 9am was number three. Although getting merry in the morning did quickly ease our symptoms, it wasn't worth the fresh hell that rolled around at 8pm with the onset of hangover number two.

Curiouser And Curiouser

The weirdest cures from around the world...

DRIED BULL PENIS
This Sicilian treatment sounds more like a cock and bull story than a delicacy.

LEMONY-FRESH ARMPIT
When life gives you lemons… stick them under your pits? Thanks for the advice, Puerto Rico.

PRAIRIE OYSTER
Oh America, why would you do this to yourself? But, in case anyone else wants to, here's the recipe...
- 1 raw egg
- 1tsp Worcestershire sauce
- 1 dash Tabasco sauce
- Salt and pepper to season
- 25ml brandy (optional)

ⓘ There's also another solution!

Swap cocktails for mocktails – turn over for some ideas that will mean the dreaded hangover doesn't even get a chance to appear.

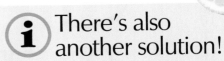

There has never been so much choice when it comes to non-alcoholic drinks – this is especially true of gin. Try some variations out, you may be in for a pleasant surprise!

Gin-Free & Tonic

Ingredients

150ml tonic water
25ml elderflower cordial
or non-alcoholic gin
15ml fresh lime juice
Cucumber slices
Lime wedges
Mint leaves
Ice cubes

Method

● Fill a glass with ice cubes.
● Add elderflower cordial or non-alcoholic gin and fresh lime juice to the glass.
● Top up the glass with tonic water.
● Stir gently to combine the ingredients.
● Garnish with cucumber slices, lime wedges and mint.

FROM ZERO TO HERO

● The rise in popularity of non-alcoholic gin reflects a broader trend towards mindful and health-conscious drinking choices. As consumer preferences shift towards wellness and moderation, non-alcoholic gin offers an enticing alternative for those seeking a sophisticated and flavourful beverage without the effects of alcohol.

● With the meticulous attention to botanicals and distillation methods that define traditional gin production, non-alcoholic gin brands craft complex and aromatic spirits that mimic the essence of gin while remaining alcohol-free.

● From botanical-infused blends to innovative distillation techniques, non-alcoholic gin provides a versatile base for creating a wide range of mocktails and alcohol-free cocktails.

You can customise this by adding a splash of vanilla extract or a shot of your favourite liqueur, such as peppermint schnapps or cinnamon whisky, for an extra kick.

Holiday Spiced Hot Chocolate

Ingredients

300ml whole milk
125ml heavy cream
5tbsp semi-sweet chocolate, chopped (or chocolate chips)
2tbsp cocoa powder
2tbsp granulated sugar (adjust to taste)
1/2tsp ground cinnamon
1/4tsp ground nutmeg
1/4tsp ground ginger
Pinch of ground cloves
Pinch of salt
Whipped cream, for topping
Ground cinnamon or cocoa powder (optional)

Method

● In a medium saucepan, combine the whole milk and heavy cream over medium heat. Heat the mixture until it starts to simmer, but do not boil.
● Reduce the heat to low, and add the chopped semisweet chocolate (or chocolate chips) to the saucepan.
● Stir continuously until the chocolate is completely melted and the mixture is smooth and creamy.
● Add the cocoa powder, granulated sugar, ground cinnamon, ground nutmeg, ground ginger, ground cloves, and a pinch of salt to the saucepan. Stir well until all the ingredients are fully incorporated.
● Continue to heat the hot chocolate mixture over a low heat, stirring occasionally, for an additional 5-7 minutes to allow the flavours to melt together and the hot chocolate to thicken slightly.
● Once the hot chocolate is heated through and thickened to your desired consistency, remove it from the heat and pour it into mugs.
● Top each mug of hot chocolate with a dollop of whipped cream.
● Garnish with a sprinkle of ground cinnamon or cocoa powder for a decorative touch.

Bellini

Ingredients
200ml peach nectar or peach puree
750ml sparkling water or soda water
Fresh peach slice
Mint leaves
Ice cubes

Method
● Chill the peach nectar or peach puree in the refrigerator.
● In a pitcher, mix the chilled peach nectar/puree with the sparkling water or soda water.
● Fill glasses with ice cubes.
● Pour the peach mixture over the ice in each glass.
● Garnish with a fresh peach slices and mint leaves
● Stir gently before serving.

Simple to make, a Bellini with prosecco or this mocktail without the alcohol is refreshing, delicious and a popular choice to serve at brunch.

Coconut Crème

Seedlip Spice & Tonic

Simple ingredients combined with a cocktail shaker and some energy to shake will leave you with this icy and creamy tropical delight!

Ingredients
50ml coconut cream
100ml pineapple juice
25ml lime juice
15ml grenadine syrup
Pineapple slice
Ice cubes

Method
● In a shaker or glass, combine the coconut cream, pineapple juice, and lime juice.
● Add ice cubes to the shaker and shake well until combined.
● Strain the mixture into a glass filled with ice.
● Slowly pour the grenadine syrup into the glass for a layered effect.
● Garnish with a pineapple slice.

This aromatic, spicy blend of botanicals offers a distinctive non-alcoholic treat with a depth and complexity similar to traditional spirits.

Ingredients
50ml Seedlip Spice 94
150ml premium tonic water
Ice cubes
Rosemary sprig
Lemon wedge

Method
● Fill a glass with ice cubes.
● Pour 50ml of Seedlip Spice 94 over the ice.
● Top it up with 150ml of premium tonic water.
● Stir gently to mix the ingredients.
● Garnish with a rosemary sprig and lemon wedge.

Shirley Temple

This drink is a regular fixture at bars for those seeking a tasty non-alcoholic beverage. Made with high-quality ingredients, it will delight even the hard-to-please!

Ingredients

150ml ginger ale
50ml lemon-lime soda
(e.g. Sprite or 7 Up)
25ml grenadine syrup
Maraschino cherry
Ice cubes

Method

● Fill a glass with ice cubes.
● Pour the ginger ale and lemon-lime soda into the glass.
● Slowly drizzle the grenadine syrup into the glass to create the signature layered effect.
● Stir gently to mix the flavours.
● Garnish with a maraschino cherry on top.

REGIONAL SPECIALTIES

Caipiroska
(Brazil)

■ Ingredients
50ml vodka
½ fresh lime, cut into wedges
2tsp sugar
Fresh mint
Ice cubes

■ Method
● Place the lime wedges in a glass and add sugar.
● Muddle the lime and sugar together to release the lime juice.
● Fill the glass with ice cubes.
● Pour vodka over the ice.
● Stir well to mix the ingredients and dissolve the sugar.
● Garnish with a lime slice and the mint.

The Caipiroska, a modern adaptation of the Caipirinha, originated in the 20th century when Brazilian travellers, missing their caçhaca, turned to vodka while overseas.

THE RIO THING!

● The Caipiroska cocktail is a must-try for cocktail enthusiasts seeking a refreshing and invigorating tropical experience.

● This cocktail revolutionises the classic recipe by elegantly substituting caçhaca with vodka, creating a smoother and more versatile flavour profile.

● With the intense citrusy punch of fresh lime wedges, the subtle sweetness of sugar, and the crisp kick of vodka, the Caipiroska concoction delivers a harmonious symphony of flavours that tantalise the taste buds.

● Enhancing its allure, the vibrant green hue of muddled limes accentuates its visual appeal. Served over ice and garnished with lime wedges, the Caipiroska stands as a delightful fusion of zesty freshness and spirited sophistication.

Michigan Cherry Old Fashioned

Inspired by the rich cherry-growing heritage of Michigan, this variation on the classic Old Fashioned (pg9) adds a unique and fruity dimension to the traditional recipe.

Ingredients
60ml bourbon
15ml cherry brandy or cherry liqueur
2-3 dashes Angostura bitters
1tsp cherry juice
Orange slice
Maraschino cherry
Sugar cube
Ice cubes

Method
● In a glass, muddle an orange slice, maraschino cherry, sugar cube and cherry juice.
● Add bourbon, cherry brandy, and Angostura bitters to the glass.
● Fill the glass with ice cubes and stir well.
● Garnish with an orange peel twist and additional cherries.

Sazerac (New Orleans)

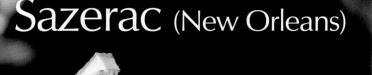

Dating back to the mid-19th century, the Sazerac cocktail is closely linked to the history of New Orleans and is even considered the official cocktail of the city.

Ingredients
60ml rye whiskey
Sugar cube
3-4 dashes Peychaud's Bitters
Absinthe or absinthe substitute
Orange slice
Ice cubes

Method
● Place a sugar cube in a mixing glass.
● Add 3-4 dashes of Peychaud's Bitters to the sugar cube.
● Crush the sugar cube and bitters together.
● Add the rye whiskey to the mixture and stir well.
● Rinse a chilled glass with absinthe or an absinthe substitute.
● Strain the whiskey mixture into the prepared glass.
● Express the oil from a lemon peel twist over the glass and garnish with the orange slice.

Tokyo Tea

Ingredients

25ml vodka
25ml rum
25ml gin
25ml tequila
25ml triple sec
25ml Midori (melon liqueur)
50ml sweet and sour mix
Lemon-lime soda
Ice cubes
Lime slice

Method

● Fill a shaker with ice cubes.
● Add vodka, rum, gin, tequila, triple sec, Midori, and sweet and sour mix to the shaker.
● Shake well to mix the ingredients. Strain the mixture into a tall glass filled with ice.
● Top up with lemon-lime soda.
● Garnish with a lemon slice.

This lime green hit is a close cousin to the Long Island Iced Tea (pg39), different by only a few ingredients, notably the melon-flavoured liqueur which gives the drink its neon colour.

Dublin Donkey

Ingredients

60ml Jameson Irish Whiskey
Ginger beer
Fresh lime juice
Lime slice

Method

● Fill a glass with ice.
● Add 60ml of Jameson Irish Whiskey to the glass.
● Squeeze fresh lime juice into the glass.
● Top up the glass with ginger beer.
● Stir gently to combine the ingredients.
● Garnish with a lime slice.

A twist on the classic Moscow Mule (pg15), the Dublin Donkey is made with Irish whiskey which makes for a delicious pairing with ginger beer.

Recipe Index

*Low-Alcohol & Mocktails